FOCUSED & ALIGNED PART II:

"THE BIRTHING ROOM"

AN ANTHOLOGY COMPILED BY
CHAUNDRA NICOLE GORE, MSL

FOCUSED & ALIGNED PART II: "THE BIRTHING ROOM"
AN ANTHOLOGY COMPILED BY CHAUNDRA NICOLE GORE, MSL

ISBN: 9798455593765

Copyright 2021 @ Chaundra Nicole Gore

Edited by: Christian Cashelle
Scriptures are from the King James Version unless otherwise specified.

Manufactured in the United States of America.

Table of Contents

Meet the Authors

Acknowledgments

The birthing process is necessary. Without it, purpose would incubate far too long. I want to give God all the glory, all the honor and all the praise for creating each one of us on purpose, with purpose. God continues to download the vision of Focused and Aligned into my spirit. I will not allow any decision to made without consulting my father God first and foremost and throughout the entire process. This anthology is not a writing project, it is a mighty move of God. The journey God has me on right now has taken me, and these ladies to greater heights. Because this project is God led, I only hired one person to assist with the processing of this book. I want to acknowledge our amazing Editor in Chief, my sister in Christ, Christian Cashelle, for always walking along side me when I ring her bell. Part II has allowed me to teach along the way and that makes this second project very powerful. I want to acknowledge every co-author on this anthology: Thank you from my heart to yours for saying yes again. May God favor each of us eternally.

Lastly, thank you to Pastor Jomo Cousins, Apostle John Eckhardt, Apostle Ryan Lestrange, Apostle Oscar Goubadia, Dr. Juanita Bynum, and Dr. Cindy Trimm for teaching me many powerful lessons on how to Master the Prophetic through your platforms. It has truly allowed me to grow in God night and day and I am grateful to each of you. The Groan gave me the ability to speak in tongues and my life has never been the same since. May God favor each of you eternally as well.

Dedication

I dedicate this book to both men and women whom have endured a struggle, trial, tribulation, or significant event in their life time. To women specifically, I want to RING the NOW bell. NOW is the time to look to the hills to whence your help comes from. Now is the time to walk by faith and not by sight. Now is the time to become FOCUSED and ALIGNED on God and not your problem.

Now is the time to connect with the people God wants you to impact and assist. Now is the time to surrender it all and allow God to use you for His purpose and plan. To everyone that has ever made a mistake in life, know this - God's grace is sufficient enough! As long as you have breath in your body, you can change the way your story ends.

Foreword

The Focused & Aligned Anthology is a mighty move of God. The vision was downloaded to me as the pandemic began. I was obedient to God and all of His instructions as He began to speak to me concerning this project specifically.

Focused from its Greek etymological root is "synkentro'no" which means to concentrate, bring together, or center. Align from its French etymological root is "ligne" meaning line, bring something in line with something else. The Focused & Aligned Anthology is a compilation of stories from Women who have walked through many trials and tribulations. These 9 Women got together and wrote about a point in their life when they realized they birthed their purpose.

In order to become focused and aligned on God, you must take intentional steps to be alone, study the word of God, meditate on the word of God, and most importantly, fast and pray. This takes you away from the crowd, away from the hustle and bustle of life and guess what else, it allows you to become very comfortable with your own company. Do you like you? You must say yes to this question in order to become focused and aligned. You must love God and understand that He is our Alpha and Omega, the beginning and the end, the author and the finisher of our faith.

As you read this amazing anthology, I want you to think about what your purpose-driven life looks like. Are you aware of what your purpose is? Are you walking in your purpose? If not, why not? What moment did you realize you had a purpose on the inside of you? Pause, ponder, and now pray about your purpose-driven life. Ask God to assist you in navigating your purpose and walking according to His will and way for your life. You must be willing to leave the old (past) behind because God creates all things new in His way. Are you open to walking a new walk and talking a new talk that allows you to be focused and aligned on God's plan and purpose for your life?

There are sacrifices that you must be willing to make in order to become focused and aligned on God. When He sees that you are walking in alignment, you are attentive to His voice and you have postured yourself to do His will and not your will, God will open the windows of heaven and pour out blessings that you will not have room enough to receive. Are you ready to be BLESSED? I know I am and it's happening for me, so take this journey with us and learn more about pushing to birth your purpose-driven life. The pain is necessary for every push to be successful. Know that God has got your back and He gave you the armor of God for your front.

Prophetess Chaundra Nicole Gore, MSL
CEO, Focused & Aligned, Lensoffaith Speaks
President, Focused and Aligned Women's
Business Empowerment Foundation Inc.

FOCUSED & ALIGNED PART II:

"THE BIRTHING ROOM"

The Birthing Process Prayer

"Now faith is the substance of things hoped for, the evidence of things not seen" Hebrews 11:1.

Heavenly Father; our Lord and Savior Jesus Christ, we want to say thank You for the completion of this book project. We thank You for allowing the visionary, Mrs. Chaundra Nicole Gore, and the co-authors who have shared their stories. Thank You for how they each weathered the storm and were able to come out victorious. God, You graced each author to complete this assignment for such a time as this. We thank You for the plans You have for our lives. For we realize that it is the Father's will that shall come to pass.

A man's heart plans his way, but the Lord directs his steps. (Proverbs 16:9) Lord, You ordered every author's steps to fulfill Your purpose. You helped them to be focused and aligned to give birth to their individual's purpose. We thank You, Lord, for the vision of this book project. We pray that each testimony shared in this book will be a blessing to others and their lives will be changed as they read these testimonies. Even though we could not see the beginning from the end, Lord you could. We put our total trust in You. Now that this book has been published, we ask that You bless this book financially as well as spiritually. We pray that our lights will shine before men so that You will be glorified. In Jesus' name.

Amen.

Minister Keywana Wright-Jones

I am a Lensoffaith

By Chaundra Nicole Gore, MSL

The moment I accepted Master Sergeant in the United States Army, it felt surreal. I was uber excited, but then the excitement quickly dwindled away. I had to make some hard choices and decisions, but not without the help of the Lord. I am screaming and shouting right now because my faith brought me to a place of understanding all that I've been through. Let me be clear, it did not feel good, but it all worked together *for* my good. Let me tell you all about it. God said, "Follow me, daughter. I'll lead the way."

Every woman that has ever been pregnant was given a due date. This is the day the baby is expected to arrive based on the day of conception or basically the day the sperm travels through the vagina, into the uterus and fertilizes an egg found in the fallopian tube. The woman then becomes pregnant with a baby that incubates for about 40 weeks, more or less. Out comes a beautiful baby, crying until it is comforted for the first time.

August 17, 2017, I received a word from the Lord to start Lensoffaith Speaks, not knowing or understanding that this very concept would take on a very prolific meaning in the near future. Inside of my small apartment in Augusta, GA, I talked to God so much that my neighbor thought I lived with someone. It was just me and God in prayer, fasting, and mediation. I had a routine that I refused to abandon. So much was happening all at once, I didn't want to become suicidal, so as my sister, Donna Hicks Izzard, would say, "I changed the picture."

I dived headfirst into my word. I sometimes sat for hours just listening to the voice of God in my prayer closet. Many days, I would get off work, lay on the floor, and just listen for God's voice. I didn't miss a beat because I didn't want to miss God. I knew He was speaking to me so I would journal and write on my sticky notes, posting them all over my apartment. I started every day with prayer, journaling, a 15-minute meditation, and I then listened to Pastor Jomo's morning message enroute to my job. I was always armed with my Bible, prayer shawl, and my anointing oil. I never left home without it. This began my close walk with God and ultimately allowed a supernatural conception to take place. My gift was being stirred up on the inside of my belly. I felt like my small apartment became my throne room, my prayer closet, my hideout, and my place of peace. After 35 years, 8 children, and a hysterectomy I was pregnant all over again.

All types of warfare began erupting in my life. My husband was cheating, the people on my job began shifting, gossip was floating through the air about me, racism was surfacing, and discrimination was all in the air. I was on a roller coaster ride to the pit...but God. This was the place that God needed me to be in to transform me into a Lens of Faith. The birthing process had begun and I had two spiritual midwives to help me push out my God-given purpose. I had to go through the crushing, the shaking, and the molding in order to get to the day in which I would push out my real purpose.

I thought that Lensoffaith was just a podcast, but God wanted to see if I would be obedient over a small thing, through the beginning of the process. God wanted to make sure I would be faithful over what He gave me and then He would elevate me to another level month by month. I followed God's instructions by looking for people that were doing amazing things in the kingdom of God. I would scroll and stop when God told me to stop. I would look at the person's profile and find out exactly what they did for the people. With care and a meticulous selection process, I prepared each week to interview a person on the Lensoffaith Speaks show. It was so much fun and very educational. I had a scripture for each episode, right along with all the questions I was going to ask on the show. I made each interviewee feel safe and welcomed. I did this for three years straight and I never charged anyone. I wanted to do it out of obedience to what God said. Love the LORD your God and keep his requirements, his decrees, his laws and his commands always (Deuteronomy 11:1).

The first sign that I was on the right track to pushing out the gift God gave me was when I was contacted by Bishop Samuel McGill III. I interviewed this powerful man of God on the Lensoffaith Speaks Show and he offered me a spot on his radio station, All Nations Stellar Award Winning Internet Radio Station. The momentum picked up and I had to not only do the talk show on Facebook Live every week, but I also had to send the recordings to Bishop to air on the radio. I was so excited, but I kept my routine of prayer, fasting, and meditation. This was the foundation of my elevation through a pit life experience. Although my military career was being juggled, I focused on God and the direction He was taking me in the midst of a very painful storm called discrimination, separation, and then divorce.

I promised God that I would not go back to 2007 when I didn't know God like I do now and tried to take my own life. This time felt different, but I felt resilient. I made sure I didn't break my routine because my blessing was in my obedience, my blessing was in my routine, my blessing was in every prayer that ascended to heaven. However, death was around me. My nephew was killed, my adopted mom died, and then my brother died. This sent triggers to my brain to go back to the suicidal ideations, but my children were also on my mind.

During this process, I was faithfully listening and watching Dr. Juanita Bynum and Dr. Cindy Trimm. These two women were game changers for me in the midst of a bad storm. I then found Apostle Ryan Lestrange and Dr. Oscar Goubadia and they helped me prophetically. I learned to war in the spirit of Elijah and Jehu. God taught my hands to war and my fingers to fight the good fight of faith. God also prompted me to start back following Apostle John Eckhardt to master the prophetic. I had an arsenal at my disposal in the realm of the spirit to break every chain and climb the mountains that were before me. I read, I watched, I studied, and I prayed. I knew that EVERYTHING HAD TO CHANGE! At the name of Jesus every knee shall bow and every tongue must confess that Jesus Christ is Lord. I was not playing with the enemy. I slayed every giant that rose up against me. However, I didn't know that He would remove me from the military, the place I loved and dedicated a lot of my time, talent, and energy. God's plan superseded my plan.

During this time, I attended the Lift, Launch, Lead book trip to the Virgin Islands and these mighty women of God prayed heaven down around me in the ocean. Let me tell you, those prayers were heard by God. They prayed for the Lord's will to be done on Earth as it is in heaven. I know that their prayers were answered because I am walking in the fullness of God right now. God has blessed me beyond measure and He is not done yet. These ladies are a part of my sister circle and they prayed me through a horrific time in my life and I am very grateful. This was truly a midwife moment I had in the realm of the spirit.

After this trip, I went back to my job and the out-process began a few months later. Every chapter of the Bible I read from Exodus to Proverbs prepared me to PUSH the baby (gift) out on the designated day, August 26, 2019. As I exited the gates of Fort Gordon Army Base, I smiled and the baby was released to breathe.

I inhaled and exhaled on the way out of a place that was filled with fear, accusations, turmoil, strife, heaviness, racism, speculation, assassination, one-sidedness, pain, no empathy, and a lack of sympathy. I discovered a system within the military that was not really for me or should I say conducive for my growth. If I could no longer deliver because of illness, sickness, and circumstance, I immediately became devalued to the leadership within the base. When I made a mistake and was deemed unfit, they immediately disowned me.

As I turned around to see the gate in the distance, I cried. Every tear that rolled down my face was a tear of joy and release knowing I could finally breathe without anyone judging me, laughing at me, or talking bad about me. I could finally breathe that baby breath that I took January 15th when I first arrived in this world. My chest began to rise and fall as I turned back around in my seat. I began to praise God for the journey that He confirmed and prepared me for. As we turned right to enter I20 to head back to Tampa, God spoke to me. "I got you. Trust me through it all."

Every choice, decision, and consequence was for my good.

The Army was my training ground to become a Soldier in the Army of the Lord. We may think that our passion is our purpose, but in reality it could be two different things. I was passionate about being a Soldier in the United States Army, but God placed me there to learn and go through some things as He prepared me to become Prophetess Chaundra Nicole Gore. In the Army I went to basic training to learn how to prepare to fight the enemy. I learned how to do physical training, shoot my weapon, gain discipline and motivation, and to grow mentally. The birthing process of becoming who God called me to be was a battle all on it's own, but what I learned in the physical Army gave me exactly what I needed to defeat every enemy in the realm of the spirit.

The word of God tells us, for we wrestle not against flesh and blood, but against principalities, powers, rulers, darkness of this world and spiritual wickedness in high places (Ephesians 6:12). The training ground I served in encompassed loyalty, duty, honor, integrity, selfless service, and personal courage. Each one of these leadership traits were needed for me to blossom and grow in order to prepare for the ultimate birthing experience of becoming Prophetess Chaundra Nicole Gore.

When I began an intentional journey studying with Dr. Cindy Trimm virtually, I learned everything about spiritual warfare. I learned that I was God's official legislator and law enforcement agent. I had to be intentional about making what was important to God, important to me so that I could advance in the direction in which He called me to go. I was able to decree and declare that in this battle no extrinsic weapon, be it emotional, financial, physical, social, psychological, spiritual, organizational, interpersonal, formed against me shall prosper. I began praying heaven down every day. I knew how to cause the enemy to flee. My prayers had direction, power, force, focus, and authority. Every word I spoke was intentional in order to direct the power and authority God gave me. Spiritual warfare is not for the weak and weary, but for the strong and mighty through God as our strong tower.

Throughout this birthing process I had to deal directly with myself. Although people were doing things to me, it was time for me to reflect on how I handled it, how I moved in it, and how I overcame it. I never wanted my mind to go back to 2007 when I tried to take my own life. I needed a new strategy, new power, and new authority to rise in me so that I could defeat the enemy on every level and dimension God was taking me to.

My strategy changed because God gave me a new perspective. My strategy changed because I shifted to focus on understanding me, working on me, and allowing God to use me for His glory. This process allowed me to give birth to a beautiful gift without the epidural. I felt every pain, every trial, and every tribulation I walked through. Psalm 23 (KJV) says, yea though I walk THROUGH! This word right here stands out to me. It tells me that I will make it to the other side. God is with me with every painful movement, every tear, and every thought of fear.

It's all about perspective for me while in the wilderness. The wilderness was my training ground, preparing me for the birthing. Without the preparation, strategy, and tactics, I would have been unaware of the different battles and what I needed for each one. My God, that's a word right there. If you only look at the battle, you forget about God. If you really look to God as your strong tower and allow God to lead the way, I promise you that through the wilderness, the lessons you learn will be very vital and valuable to your success. We all were created with purpose. Know that God has your back because He has given you the armour for your front. He won't allow you to fail when you make what's important to Him, important to you. He will then make what's important to you, important to Him. God wants your time and undivided attention so that you can birth the best thing that has ever happened to you-YOUR PURPOSE. You must go through the Birthing Process, in order to get to the manifestation of the GIFT on the INSIDE of YOU! NOW, PUSH!

A Leader in Vitro

Birthing my business during COVID-19

By Charlene Harrod-Owaumana, AAS, LPN

It started with a friend giving information about women's leadership certification. Given by eCornel; sponsored by Bank. I will be taking you on my journey as it takes place in real time. Yes, real time. The outcome will be from the two (2) month study period and where I landed after the program. So sit back, grab your favorite drink, and relax in a comfortable chair in a warm, dimly lighted area. Watch the Birthing Process and Journey come to fruition – in Leadership and Influencing the Influencer.

True Leadership

True leadership cannot be built on our accomplishments. It cannot be selfish, where we look and value the materialistic things in life. There are major things we must have if we are going to follow God. We must have denial ability; we have to be able to deny our fleshly desires and what we want for ourselves. We have to give up pride. We have to deny ourselves and think of others. Sharing the gifts that God gave us with others is important. Take up His cross and follow Him. What are you willing to give up for the Lord? Are you willing to deny yourself and kill your desires to make sure you are leading by example? Show that you are a true Leader to those you have influence over.

Leadership is defined by the level of Influence you have on others. It's not in the certificates that you receive; it's not in the doctorates you receive. It's all about how you leverage your Influence; make someone else's life better. First - one will have to deny themselves. Secondly - have to be willing walk a certain way. In order to be effective in our Leadership we have to not be selfish in our service but selfless in His will. We have to carry a level of Influence; so we can let others know that it is important to have influence to effectively impact someone else's life. True Leadership does not wait for their name to be called. True Leadership will want their work to speak on there behalf. What level of Influence do you have on someone else LIFE?

Level of Influence

True Leadership has to be earned. You cannot buy time to increase your influence. But one would have to be really careful not to undermine others. Some folks can see and read between lines. Just because someone either went to college or obtained a degree where they were able to add letters behind their name - does not mean that they are a leader. Leading a team requires you to influence, not manage them.

Here are several factors that will influence the influencers:

CHARACTER - True character begins with oneself and filters throughout the organization.

RELATIONSHIP - Build and develop deep relationships within organizations with people who believe in your mission. This grows the business in many ways; such as: loyalty and influencing others.

KNOWLEDGE - Before working for any organization; do your research, learn the organization and find out what they are missing and come up with a solution. Knowledge is Power!!!

INTUITION - Find out what is needed to impact the organization and present your findings in a professional way.

EXPERIENCE -   Take your past and present obstacles and re-evaluate them. This will have a lasting effect on your followers and ultimately build respect.

PAST SUCCESS - Do not guarantee future success. Finding ways to overcome challenges will help build new responsibilities and leadership opportunities.

ABILITY - Leading your organization and team to victory is the ultimate goal.

Using your knowledge will take you a long way in your business and/or organization. This will give your influencers a positive role model to follow. This also shows your true leadership skills. Below are some questions to ask yourself.

1. Where are you on your Leadership Journey?
2. Everyone wants to know where they stand in their Leadership Journey and how can they go to the next level. Explain your Leadership Journey and what's your next step?
3. Of the factors listed above, which one should your company invest in the most?
4. Write down in order, how you can be a better influencer in your organization/business:

Living & Dying in the Transition

By Melannie F. Hines

Childbirth is a violent event. There is stretching, tearing, blood, sweat, and tears. Entering the world to walk in your purpose is also a painful process. Since we can only speculate what a baby feels as they make the journey down the birthing canal, in my imagination, the baby is confused because something is happening that has never happened before. What was at one point the warmest, most comfortable, and safest place for the baby to be has become hostile and dangerous as they are squeezed through a narrow space that, if stuck in the transition, could die. Now, many other challenges can occur during childbirth. However, I want to talk about the transition because I was born in that time and space.

My life was a series of transitions growing up in an active-duty military family. Every three or four years, I was required to uproot what I thought was an irreplaceable life; leave all of my best friends, and worst of all, be without my toys for the month it took for us to pack everything and ship it to the new place. At that point in my life, I thought that traveling around the world for my dad's job would be the most impactful part of my life considering it dictated everything I did. Surprisingly enough, God had a different plan. I was born a singer. In fact, as a child, it was the only thing I could do. My sister was the pretty and smart one, my brother was the cool and handsome one, and I was a terrible student in the special education math class. If I was chosen at all, I was picked last to be on anyone's team. I was the little girl who the boys gave notes to see if I would ask my friend if she liked him.

Fast forward to middle school, yet another transition. I moved from England to the United States at the age of 12. I got into trouble in class and spent the better part of those years with better attendance in the in-house suspension classroom than I did in my actual classes, but it was during this time that I discovered my passion for music and my love for God. Not only was I born to be a singer, but I was born to sing, write, and lead. How does this all relate to childbirth, you ask? Let me explain. It was during the years that I began to develop my musical talents that I started to separate myself from all of the things that were comfortable to me. I didn't really like singing in front of people, but something happened inside the womb of purpose and I couldn't hold the music in anymore. I began singing in front of people and they liked it! It didn't matter that I wasn't as pretty as my sister or as cool as my brother. All anyone cared about was that I could sing.

Please don't misunderstand; things didn't magically turn around for me at that point; I continued to get kicked out of school, sent to the dean's office, and get bad grades. Apparently, the teachers didn't care that I could sing. By the time I reached my last year in middle school, the dean told me the only reason he was allowing me to transition to the 9th grade was because he didn't want me in his school anymore. That didn't matter to me because I had shared the stage with the industry elite by that time, and I knew I would be famous before I graduated high school. I won't bore you with the details of high school; but know that I was still singing, my grades were still pretty mediocre, but I was not getting kicked out of school anymore.

As an adult, I dropped out of college and continued singing, performing, sharing Christ with others, and writing. I continued to meet and be mentored by people I had been a fan of my whole life, and in my mind, I had arrived. I consider this part of my story Braxton hick's contractions. My body and mind thought something was happening but, in actuality, it was a false alarm.

Drinking, sex, and music were my comfort. The drinking was to numb my mind so I could ignore how I felt about myself; the sex was to feel something other than the overwhelming pain of loneliness, and the music, well, that was my safe place and my therapy. After realizing that I was not any further along than when I got to Los Angeles, I moved back home to Las Vegas, NV, with my parents. I continued to sing and perform, except now I had a chip on my shoulder that caused me to walk into venues with a"do you know who I am?" attitude. It didn't help that people did know who I was. DJs would announce when I would walk in and I could grab the mic and get on stage anywhere I went with no debate or questions asked. Disillusioned, the purpose inside me had stopped growing and I passed my due date because I failed to go into labor. Local celebrity falsely elevated me to a place in my mind where I could not see that I had not made it to the destination, and in fact, my purpose was dying because I did not transition. My purpose was lying dormant when I should have been giving birth.

In the meantime, I became involved with a man who was married but separated and abusive. We were homeless on many occasions; living in a friend's car or moving from one friend's house to another. We would pretend to be employees of different casinos to get a meal for the day in their cafeterias. A transition came. We moved in with his mother and entered the system of government assistance. I kept saying to myself, *what are you doing, Melannie? You didn't grow up like this!* We eventually joined a church and I thought I was finally going to be born. However, while singing in the choir and leading the praise and worship team, I was being abused physically, mentally, and emotionally. I could not see a way out. I kept everything that I was going through to myself because I was embarrassed. I was still attempting to sing, but the horror show I called my life snuffed out any chance of purpose being birthed. For the first time in my life, people told me I could not sing. The person who was supposed to be my biggest supporter served as an abortion clinic. Aborting dream after dream, I lost all confidence in myself and my gift. I went back to being the ugly duckling in elementary school that had no friends and no talents or gifts. I was lost, terrified, alone, and in pain.

I began to feel God pulling on me, telling me that I needed to make a change and that a transition was coming. The labor pains began! The Lord told me where He was going to take me and to get rid of everything. I could not take anything from this life with me. The Lord led me to Genesis 12:1, where he said to Abram, "Leave your native country, your relatives, and your father's family, and go to the land that I will show you." I didn't know what it meant or how it would happen because we didn't have any money. A few weeks later, a family member called and said that we should move in with them to help each other. God had already prepared the way and I didn't even know it! Another family member called and said we should move with them because they had a studio and we could tap into what God had for us, so we moved again.

I became depressed. Most days, I would not come out of the room. I read scriptures to help build my faith and pull myself out of where I was, but all of the scriptures kept talking about the Army of the Lord and being a soldier. So, I did what I believed the Lord was telling me to do. I went to a recruiting station when the Army had people on a waiting list to "ship" to Basic Training, but God had a different plan for me. Transition. I signed my contract and enlisted in the Army Reserves on August 8th, 2012 and was shipped off to Basic on the 16th. The recruiters all said that I was the quickest ship to ever come out of that recruiting station. I completed Basic and AIT as a leader favored by my leadership.

Transition. My family was alerted to what was going on in my marriage. I was free! I was now in the delivery room with my family and friends surrounding me, coaching me through labor, breathing with me, and holding my hand. Transition. I got my apartment, became legally separated to file for divorce, worked three jobs, and joined a band. Everything was going great and then I received the best gift. I was accepted to the Active Guard Reserve program. At that time, I reconnected with my high school sweetheart. I got stationed in Grand Prairie, Texas; 45 minutes from where he lived. I knew that it was a sign from God that he and I were meant to be together. I would make jokes and say that we needed to just get married, and eventually, it became a reality but not before one of the most terrifying transitions of my life.

In December 2014, a driver of a black SUV ran a light, crashing into the driver side of my tiny Chevy Sonic. All I could think of at that moment was that I was going to die, but God had a different plan for me that night. Waking up in the hospital, my soon-to-be husband was at my side. I was bedridden for what seemed like forever. I could not bathe myself, fix my food, or go to the bathroom by myself. It was a very humbling experience for me. After being released from bed rest, I was on crutches for about six months to learn how to stand up straight while being taught how to walk without support. I felt helpless. I was the heaviest I had been in years and I felt unattractive. My man was attentive and made sure I got what I needed. Despite the weight gain, he still loved me as I made efforts to heal and regain strength and mobility. Transition. I am now off crutches, my boyfriend and I are engaged, and I sink back into what I thought would be the deepest depression. My mood changed, I couldn't sleep, and of course, my relationship suffered. Now the real contractions begin. My behavior became so erratic that the leadership in my unit ordered me to go to a mental health professional. In the meantime, I am losing time and isolating myself; I stopped singing and performing. I am still in constant pain, overweight, and feeling undesirable, so I shut down emotionally, sexually, musically, and spiritually.

Transition. The cervix is dilating more. I am barely breathing, so I focus on something else in the room that is not painful. I become the best at my job, working as hard and as much as possible, receiving the validation and satisfaction that my personal life does not offer. The Army says it's time to move again. Transition. It is almost time to push. I continue to dominate at work yet fail at home. I make plans with friends and cancel them, afraid to go outside. Nobody sees the broken woman in front of them because I am so good at pretending.

In 2019, I was deployed to Iraq. I am doing what I'm trained to do and I love it! There were rocket attacks regularly, but you reach a point where you hear it and you lay in your bed numb to the overwhelming fear. *If this is how I die, at least I'll be warm in my bed.* Now joining my sex drive, spirituality, and emotions in the off position are empathy and compassion. I am no longer breathing. Another contraction.

In November 2019, a rocket attack left me with permanent pain and damage to my right hand. I arrived home in December 2019 and the world looks different. I can't sleep, food tastes different, and I can't adjust to being home. Contraction. Having a baby is taken off the table. My husband no longer wants to do IVF and does not know if he still wants to be married to me. January 2020, I get back to work thinking that I will finally be in a familiar place. Contraction, I am almost fully dilated. I can't adjust at work either. My relationship is hanging on by a thread and the one thing that I knew I could focus on was gone. The head of my purpose begins to crown, but the contractions begin to slow down and get further apart. Being a wife, mother, singer, writer, and performer are no longer options. I lay on the couch terrified of loud noises as I hallucinate because I haven't slept in days. I was alone in a dark place and at times death seemed like the only way out.

My purpose is now suffocating in the transition. I moved to Omaha NE in July 2020 alone with my purpose dying a painful death inside me. Thinking a change of scenery will help, I do my best to be the soldier I know I can be. I am blessed with things. A house, a car, a good-paying job during a pandemic while people are losing their jobs and loved ones. I am secretly losing the internal fight of my life. The fear is unbearable. I sit in my car agonizing over how I need to just end it all because I have nothing left. I am struggling at this point even to exist. The water is too deep and I am sinking. I am alone in a world where we have sayings like "the world is your oyster" and "there is somebody for everybody." I must not belong in this world because this is not my reality. Just as I decided to quit, God stepped in and walked me through His word daily. My eyes were opened. It's like stepping out of a bunker after the world has been decimated. Looking at what seems like irreparable damage, I tried to restore broken relationships only to be met with the reality that I've been the one who has been asleep all this time and the world has moved on without me.

God's word started the contractions again, the head came out, and the darkness became light. Still struggling to breathe, I grasped for any glimpse of life I could find. Another contraction comes and God says to push. The shoulder, arms, and hands came out. The baby's chest is exposed and there is a heartbeat. It is weak, but it is there. I begin writing and recording again. Contraction. God allows me to see who I have been in my marriage over the years and how hurtful my actions were. I fell in love with my husband all over again and desperately tried to regain his trust. Contraction. He has moved on.

God tells me to push. I acknowledge that I was homeless, abused, and on welfare for a reason. Isaiah 10:1-3 NIV, "Woe to those who make unjust laws, to those who issue oppressive decrees, to deprive the poor of their rights and withhold justice from the oppressed of my people, making widows their prey and robbing the fatherless. What will you do on the day of reckoning when disaster comes from afar? To whom will you run for help? Where will you leave your riches?" By faith, my doctoral degree will put me in the room with lawmakers to help change welfare policies for the better.

One final push. It is a challenge for me to live daily. In March 2021, I was diagnosed with PTSD, adding it to an already long list of disorders. I believe God allowed me to survive the attack in Iraq and is helping me to survive the attack on my mind to share my story to help others choose life every day. My purpose was born out of chaos, heartbreak, trauma, and pain. I have been stretched to the point of being ripped apart. I have bent to the point of breaking. I cried until I had no tears left. As I said, childbirth is a violent event.

You Can Run, but You Can't Hide

By Pastor Darlene Hopkins Thorne, MDiv

I ran from my purpose. I didn't think that God could use me. I thought my life was way too terrible for Him to want to use me. I was the daughter of pastors. Yes, the preacher's kid. I heard the word, I knew what the word meant, I understood what it meant to be called by God, and yet, I ran. Why did I run?

I watched my parents' relationship crumble and fall after 23 years of marriage. I watched them go through nights of arguing, fighting and then walked into church services and watched my mother play the organ from the depths of her heart while singing, "It took a Miracle." I watched my father preach messages that changed and transformed so many people's lives. They were on the altar, crying, weeping, and asking God for forgiveness. I was the daughter of a failed marriage. Little did I know that this was a part of the design God had for me. When my parents split, I lived with my mother, my two older sisters, and my younger brother. We were all there, living a nightmare. Hearing voices of people who talked about us, yet they smiled in our faces. I felt as though there was nothing for me to even live for.

Many times, I attempted to take my own life. I didn't think I was worthy of living. If my parents couldn't survive a relationship, what would my future hold? I know it might sound strange to some of you, but I was only 15 years old and I had no understanding of what it really meant. My parents weren't splitting because of me or my siblings, it was because of their own inability to work out their relationship. But at 15, what did I know? So, for the next three or four years, I took my mother through a living hell. I was promiscuous. I was disobedient. I did everything within my power to drown out the noise of God calling me. I did everything I could to live my life without God as my Savior. But, oh how wrong I was.

I looked for acceptance from false friends. In school I was teased because of my skin complexion. The same girls I went to church with pretended to be my friend on Sundays and called me names like Blackie and Midnight Monday through Friday. My parents taught me to turn the other cheek. When I told my mother about how I was being treated, her response was, "Sticks and stones may break my bones, but words will never hurt me." That was the biggest untruth! Words hurt! Every day I dreaded going to school because of the name calling and threats of getting into unwanted fights. But in all of this, God had a plan!

My life was not going in the direction that I thought it would. When I got teased, I tried so desperately to fit in. I became a people pleaser. Anything I could do to be accepted. How many of us know that when God has a calling on your life you will not be accepted by those who do not love Him? In our home we were not allowed to wear pants. Somehow, I came across some pants and hid them in my schoolbag. I got to school and changed thinking that was going to get me to be a part of the in group. That only made things worse. They knew I was going to have to take them off before I got on the bus to go home. I was humiliated.

During one summer, I remember attending a conference. During that conference, the teacher, Bill Gothard, talked about honoring our parents even when they're wrong. I was 18 years old. I sat and I listened to this man talk to us about how we will stand before God by ourselves and have to give an account for what He placed in us individually.I began to think about what I did when I was 12 years old. I preached my very first sermon. I remembered singing with my sisters and even writing some music. I remembered writing poetry. Memorizing scripture came easy to me as a young girl.

We participated in Bible bowls where we would quote scriptures that we memorized and I won so many trophies. We would also have relays in who could find the scripture in the Bible first. And I remember again, before the age of 15, winning because I knew these verses, or as a young child, again, 10 years old, sitting on the steps in our house, reading from cover to cover the Bible. Yes, it was the Living Bible, the children's version, however, what child at 10 or 11 years old was reading the Bible? As I recalled all of these things that I did before the age of 15, and then I'm 18 years old, having run from God, running from Him, running from the call that was on my life.

I remember leaving the conference, running in the rain toward the hotel to call my mother. I was weeping and wailing uncontrollably. I could barely see to dial the numbers. As I called my mom and she answered the phone, all I could do was wail, cry, scream, and holler. "I'm so sorry. I'm so sorry. I disobeyed you, Mommy, I'm so sorry. I disappointed you, Mommy, I'm so sorry."

I heard her on the other line telling me how much she loves me and how much she has been praying for me every day. She had been laying on the floor, prostrating, crying out to God for me because she knew that there was a call of God on my life.

And even to this day, I remember hearing my mother crying out to the Lord in the wee hours of the morning. She would be praying and interceding on our behalf saying, "Lord, keep my children. Lord, bless them. Don't let them rest until they serve you with their whole heart."

Now, I am not going to tell you that life was easy after that first YES to God! There have been continual encounters where I struggled with saying yes. Those yeses meant another layer of surrender, another death to my fleshly desires.

Even after I had said yes to the Lord and surrendered my life to Him, I still had to be delivered from my own issues because of the things I endured as a young girl. Although I was serving God, I did not realize that without truly being totally sold out to God I was still living beneath my privileges. Without the confidence I needed to have, I would shrink back and not move fully in the gifts God had placed in me. Because of doubt and fear there was a glass ceiling I was not able to break through.

I still had to face my own inadequacies and understand that it was not about what I could do but about what God would do through me. As God's chosen vessel to do what He has designed for me to do, it is a daily laying down of my life for Him to live big in me. I had to become the hands and feet of Jesus. Nothing of true value comes easy and in order to move forward the cost has to be counted.

My defining moment came when I was at an all night prayer service. I was praying and crying out to God, telling Him that I didn't want to keep living in fear. I was tired of not having all I knew I was supposed to have from God. This time I was not going to leave that church building without being free! I remember laying before the Lord and telling Him I needed to be delivered. It was at that moment that one of the brothers came and laid hands on my head and began to prophesy over my life. As he spoke, tears welled up in my eyes and I cried out and it was as if there was a weight that had once been laying on me left! I laid out on that floor feeling the Holy Spirit do an internal operation on my heart. When I got up, I felt like I had lost 10 pounds.

I began to write in my journal what God had spoken to me while I laid at His feet. He told me who I was and what I had in Him. That was my rebirth. When I got up I was convinced that there was nothing that would stop me from being the teacher, pastor, and preacher that God has called me to be.

As I reflect on why I am sharing my story, I remember sitting in the car with my mom one day and she said, "Darlene, you know you should write a book about your life. I believe people would be blessed to hear your story. There's so much you have to share. There is so much God has placed in you that they need to hear."

Even though she did not live to see my first book published, I know that she is rejoicing. I know she is grateful. I know she is thankful that I carried out what she asked me to do, to write about my story, my journey to now being a coach and author, a speaker. My husband and I serve as pastors in a home-based ministry. The two of us stand side by side, preaching the good news of the gospel without apology. We have said yes to God. After 36 years of marriage, my husband and I are more committed than ever to carry out the call of God that is on our lives.

Growth in Motion

Author Twanita S. Lassiter, Poet

Have you had the urge to be more than you are? The urge to do more than the minimum? Have you ever felt like you were missing the mark, not fulfilling a purpose-your purpose? Let's talk about it! You visualize and dream about a version of yourself that possess ALL of the traits and characteristics that you desire to project. He or she is the total package and you want to display this TRUE version of yourself but it takes GROWTH IN MOTION. In order to have growth in motion you must be willing and able to do three things: speak, write, and pray. By now you may be wondering how you achieve growth in motion by speaking, writing, and praying? The best response I can provide you as an example is my story. Pay close attention so you do not miss a gem, nugget, or jewel.

1. Speak IT into existence: Walk by faith, not by sight.

Sounds cliché, and oftentimes dismissed, but it is possible.
In 2013, I attended the Women of Faith Conference that spearheaded several pivotal events in my life. While listening to several phenomenal, inspirational speakers, a jolt of excitement came over me and, in that moment, I knew I wanted to be an inspirational speaker. Once the excitement dissipated, my faculties realigned and I remembered how much I disliked being the center of attention. However, I could not shake the feeling of helping others.

On the last day of the conference, I walked by a vendor table that happened to be a book publishing company. To set a timeline for you, the event was roughly 3 to 4 days in length and I had to enter and exit through the same door to reach my assigned seat for the entire duration. I did not notice this table until the last day. The vendor table is significant because I had just graduated with my master's degree and decided I needed something else to do and that I would write a book. The thought of writing a book was more than a one time occurrence prior to seeing the table. I spoke about it on more than one occasion: poem selection and location, chapter titles, and the title of the book. Noticing the vendor table was my opportunity to carpe diem and I did just that. I did not know how I was going to pay for this endeavor but I moved forward in pursuit of my goal and walked by faith and not by sight. Guess what? The publishing company offered a payment plan and my journey began. It took time, two years to be exact, to move from paper and pencil to digital with well over 50 poems. In April 2015, I published my first collection of poetry, *Poetree Growth In Motion*, and I have been excelling ever since.

Everything you do in life starts with a thought.

2. Write IT out: Get comfortable with being uncomfortable.

I have always been a quiet person and avoided the spotlight. Being the center of attention makes me uncomfortable. I am talking about perspiration (underarms, hands and under breast; disgusting!) and shakiness (hands and voice). Becoming the center of attention would make me shrink, especially if I was not engaged in an activity that required me to do so. Oddly enough, my strong dislike fueled me to become intentional with actions to meet objectives and goals that I set for myself. Here is how it came to pass.

In August 2015, my family and I relocated to Augusta, Georgia from Washington, DC and our immediate family was a few hours away. I was no longer on a mental and spiritual journey but also a physical one. Every aspect of my life was NEW: job, community, associates, and friends. With everything being new, I decided to dive right in and try something else new as well. I attended my first faith-based vision board party in January 2016. I had to drive from Augusta to Atlanta and this was no easy feat. Let me tell you, I was about to throw in the towel. My face was stained with tears, my body overcome with frustration, panic, and defeat as I was turned around and lost in this foreign city on my first trip. I called the hostess several times for her to guide me to the location. Just when all hope was lost and I was going to head back to Augusta, by the grace of God, I found her. I sat at a table with bright, shining faces as the room flowed with love and positivity, I could feel God in the room. Here is where it gets GOOD! As I cut out words and pictures, I heard God say, "You will be an inspirational speaker" as my hand was drawn to words such as woman speaker, inspiration, and public speaking. My response to God was apprehension.

"Are you sure?" I asked God.

I stood up and shared what had been placed on me and received strong encouragement. I took notes and wrote down actions that I could take to assist me in achieving my goal of becoming an inspirational speaker.

The following week, I shared my dislike of public speaking with my co-worker and he introduced me to Toastmasters International. Toastmasters International assists with improving public speaking, communication, and leadership skills. I became intentional with my actions and became a member of Toastmasters International to improve my public speaking skills. I increased my participation in open mic events to get comfortable with being uncomfortable. My intentionality forced me to become the version of myself that I visualized.

We have all heard the phrase, write the vision; make it plain. Well, I did that with a twist. Details are important to me. It is great to see the end game but it is more important to have the details of how you are going to attain the vision along the way.

Everything that you do in life starts with a thought, that thought becomes a vision.

3. Pray about IT.

God is full of surprises! As I walked on my journey of intentionality in 2016, I began to have dreams and thoughts of starting a business. The thoughts intensified and I began to speak about it to my husband and a few close friends. God was preparing me to venture into uncharted territory again. To be honest, the thought of a business terrified me because it was not something I had thought about before. Nonetheless, I conducted research on how to start a business, how to create a business plan, and a limited liability company versus a corporation. I began to write out a detailed plan of action. I was unclear of exactly what the purpose of the business would be so I had to PRAY and pray hard.

This particular journey was not an easy one because self-doubt was real and ever present. I did not view myself as qualified to complete the tasks before me. I had moments when I questioned myself and God once I knew the purpose.

"Who am I to think I can lead people to a better version of themselves? Who am I to guide people through their emotional turmoil? God, I do not have the credentials."

Through prayer and conversation with God, I learned to ask different questions and change my mindset. My questions and statements evolved into optimism, confidence, and reassurance.

"Who am I to think that I am not qualified? God, thank You for using me for Your kingdom. I AM ENOUGH. I AM QUALIFIED. I AM FEARFULLY AND WONDERFULLY MADE."

Walking by faith, not by sight and being intentional in my actions allowed me to birth a business. Poetree Growth In Motion, LLC focuses on growth in motion through therapeutic writing, vision board workshops, and youth conferences. Prayer and obedience led and continues to lead the way. During prayer you must remember that it is literally a two-way conversation. You must be specific; listen twice as much as you speak and give thanks for what is and what is to come. God plants the seed, provides us with the gift, and lays out resources. Our only job is to follow through in obedience.

Growth does not occur when you are comfortable. Growth occurs when you are out of your comfort zone. Do it afraid!

Everything that you do in life starts with a thought; that thought becomes a vision; that vision becomes reality.

Overcoming Adversity

When living a life of intentionality, you are bound to face adversity. Adversity may be self-imposed, intrapersonal relationships, or environmental in nature. Self-imposed adversity is the negativity you place on yourself. It may be a thought or a question of your authority on your journey. You have read examples of my self-destruction including questioning God, writing, speaking, or thinking of death in my ability to move forward in my God-given purpose. To combat negative self-talk I had to change the narrative and my perspective. I achieved this goal with prayer but also by establishing POSITIVE AFFIRMATIONS. An affirmation is the process of affirming or being affirmed, emotional support, and encouragement. I wrote several affirmations confirming who I am in Christ. I recited my affirmations in the mirror daily looking myself square in the eyes.

Sometimes with tears and other times with a huge smile of reassurance in who I am in Him. Speaking life into oneself is not an easy feat depending on the level of fear encountered. Rest assured, when you change your thoughts, you change your reality.

Intrapersonal relationships are just as impactful as an interpersonal relationship. The phrase *"sticks and stones may break my bones but words will never hurt me"* is misleading, a bold face lie. The weight of words can be relentless, a seemingly permanent fixture in life. The negativity, discouragement, and disbelief from others in your ability to accomplish the task God has placed on you can linger for years if not addressed. How do you address it? For starters, remove yourself from the negative talk because it is counterintuitive to the personal affirmations recited on a daily basis. Second, practice forgiveness. Once you forgive those who may have harmed you, bludgeoned you with their words or nonverbal actions; intentionally or unintentionally, you allow yourself to be free. You are free from the thoughts of others that somehow became your own, you are free to choose to love yourself, and you are free to walk alongside God because your burdens are light. Forgiveness allows you to move towards the version of yourself you wish to project to the world.

The world – environmental adversity. Environmental adversity consists of stereotypes or unrealistic goals society thrusts upon you creating a feeling of inadequacy. One way to combat environmental adversity is to visualize your desires and goals. Visualization assists in taking steps to present your authentic self to the world. This is accomplished by creating a vision board with detailed steps on how to reach your objective and prayer. *Matthew 7:7-8, "Ask and it will be given to you; seek and you will find; knock and the door will be opened to you. For everyone who asks receives; he who seeks finds; and to him who knocks, the door will be opened."* Follow through and your vision will become reality.

Growth in motion.

I Can't Stop Now

Author Mia Monique

How did I even get here? Thrusted on the frontline, telling my story, sharing so candidly what I felt at the time broke me and hurt me so deeply. There were many days I struggled with hiding, running, and faking it until I made it because that is what I was accustomed to. It was not until I realized I couldn't stop, that a fierce, powerful woman of God emerged. I not only emerged, but I also arrived. I realized that faith had the power to propel me to the highest mountains. My faith in God would be the key component to my purpose.

I want to teach every listening ear how I overcame tragic circumstances and let them know they can, too. It is my sole mission to share my testimony to every person who comes to me, who depends on me. I owe it all to that younger Mia that suffered. I owe it all to God to use His word and grace to tell others how He spared my mind and my life. I am firmly planted into my purpose.

What is my purpose? My purpose is to use my story and my experiences of overcoming life's obstacles by applying faith and positive thinking. My purpose is to teach my methods of manifestation, worship, the power of positive thinking, and inspired action to those who seek to live a healed and whole life. After all, I am focused and aligned. My experiences have qualified me with a master's degree in adversity. I have not passed every test however, I am an honor student in this game of life and it is not over. I know that there is nothing too big for God and that is how I became focused and aligned.

When I shared my story in *Focused and Aligned; an Anthology*, I was merely sharing. I had grown and begun to come out of my shell. I decided that I would leave the realm of fear and procrastination and answer the call of the Lord which was for me to get focused and aligned with my purpose. I had run so long, I let the enemy use my fear and pain as a tool to hold me back. However, I knew that everything I had experienced was not in vain. How could I not share my testimony? How could I not share the goodness that God has done in my life? How could I not lead by example? So, once I accepted that and walked in that, I began to teach myself consistency so I could remain focused.

What truly helped me overcome domestic abuse, depression, and fear of evolving was applying manifestation using the law of attraction into my day-to-day activities. I used words of affirmation and meditation to strengthen my mind. It was not easy coming to this place. I remember the day I decided that a change needed to happen. It was April 9th, 2019, a hot sunny morning in Cleveland, Ohio. I packed up what I could fit in my car and me and my youngest Son set out for Tampa, Florida. That was a long fifteen-hour drive filled with so many emotions. Looking back, I think I cried for four straight hours. I made the grueling decision to leave my family, my grandkids, and my friends. It was not an easy decision, it was necessary. I did not know what was in store for me, I just knew that I needed to do it.

We made it to Florida in the wee hours of the morning. Aside from all the bad, it felt good to be at our destination. I had a plan to get settled, find us a place, and make a new life. After all the times I had tried to get myself focused and aligned, I just was not. I was completely out of alignment with everything. My mental, physical, and emotional state were all out of whack, from the highs and lows of life as I knew it. I was determined to create change and leaving Ohio for good was the foundation I set to do so. So, here I was in Tampa; new city, new job, no friends, and nothing to do but set the groundwork for this new birth impregnated into my spirit. I was ready.

My favorite scripture I often meditate on is Jeremiah 29:11. "For I know the plans I have for you, declares the LORD, 'plans to prosper you and not to harm you, plans to give you hope and a future'." I recited that verse over and over until I had it memorized. I made connections with like minded women and gentlemen who inspired me to keep going and believing and before I knew it, I was speaking out more, using my methods of manifesting to create the life I wanted.

I met with our visionary, Chaundra Nicole Gore, on Thanksgiving 2019. I learned we had so much in common. Her story, like mine, was so compelling and touching. We spoke and I explained to her my desires and my passions and immediately she encouraged me to continue to seek God and believe in my purpose. As I expressed in *Focused and Aligned; an Anthology*, it was a great longing inside of me to share my story and show how I overcame all the obstacle's life threw at me. I would overcome them over and over if I had to. One thing I learned to accept is that when you are living a life of purpose there will be obstacles, there will be challenges. The fact is the bigger the obstacle, the bigger the reward. Learning to change my mindset was my biggest hurdle. We often tend to hold on to old belief systems and habits, however the beauty in a changed mind is like driving in a brand new car, the smell, the cleanliness, the purity of that is unmatched.

Chaundra invited me to participate in the anthology and life for me was never the same. I applied my manifestations into a journal that I wrote into daily. I listed everything I wanted to achieve. A book, a home, new furniture, a Mercedes Benz, a Podcast, an organization, and happiness. I wrote these down and I cut out special pictures to symbolize the meaning of each goal. I prayed over that book and read it daily. I could not believe my eyes as I went over that list and realized I had achieved all those goals within two years. Now, I am the host of my own podcast. I have a magazine, made a best-seller list, and created a manifestation group which encourages other women and men who want to achieve their dreams to apply the principles of law of attraction and journaling. I believed in myself, I took inspired action, and I created connections with people who shared the same passions as me and life could not be easier.

It's amazing how a change of environment and circle can benefit you in ways that are so unbelievable, making your life unrecognizable. What I do know is that none of this could have happened had I not taken a chance, had I not gotten tired of feeling beat down and unfulfilled. Had I not applied faith and trusted God with my life, I would not be where I am today. Today, I have principles I live by such as consistency and dedication. Today, I do not live in fear, I live in faith. Today, I am walking with my head high and heart so full of God's love that I want to share it with people who share similar stories. I talk about issues with abandonment, loneliness, and hopelessness. I encourage my following and clients to unpack their baggage and sort through the mess. Giving them hope with transparency and encouragement is the guidance and love we are taught through our father and his son, Jesus Christ. I also encourage myself.

I fell in love with the new woman created on April 9, 2019. I am just getting started, but off to the greatest start. I made a deal with God that hot April day that I can't stop and I will not. I vowed to change my life and inspire others to do the same and that is what I do. My organization, Meaningful Impact Association, equips women, men, and young adults with the necessary tools to overcome traumas they have faced with counseling, self-esteem building, and group exercise activities. I firmly believe that what we grow through are tests that ultimately end up being our testimonies. The pain and traumas I survived made me an expert and a guide to help others do the same. I will forever be grateful for the seed of life and second chances God placed inside of me. It has birthed a beautiful new thing in Christ Jesus. I have arrived.

I Didn't Know I was Pregnant

By Prophetess Mont'ique "Honeybee" Moore

"How could I not know I was pregnant?" The woman inquires to herself as she begins to give labor unexpectedly in an unprepared space. One woman thought she was constipated and actually gave birth inside her toilet bowl; another thought she had bad cramps and delivered her baby on an airplane. The laundry list of questions that continue to accompany these miraculous births tend to be more doubtful than congratulatory. However, although my experience wasn't as dramatic as these stories, it was similar in many ways. I found myself unexpectedly birthing a purpose that I didn't even know existed, which we will get into more later in this chapter. I compare my purpose-path to the unexpected pregnancy, the one when you are walking around for seven to nine months completely unaware that a baby is even growing inside of you then suddenly contractions start or your water breaks. Unbelievable right? Well believe it, this happens more often than we think.

Having a baby and becoming a mom is a desired goal many women have throughout their lives. When I was a little girl, I played with my dolls all the time, nurturing, dressing, feeding, and loving them. I adored my baby dolls so much that I knew one day I would become a mother for real. Like many others, I planned my future. I knew that I had to go to school, so I projected that after college and my big career was in the bag, I would be married and pregnant by age 28. Yup! I had this whole life thing figured out by the time I was 11 years old, so I thought. When I think back to those times and those plans I laugh at myself, not because it wasn't a good plan just that I never planned for the unexpected things that happened instead.

I actually had my first daughter when I was 18 years old, unmarried, fresh out of high school, and with no career direction. I guess you can say, I fell three goals and ten years short of my plan. My godfather used to always tell me, "You have great ideas Goddaughter, now show God your plans and watch Him show you His." I didn't get what he was saying at first but many years later it began to make so much sense.

We make plans and set goals for what seems best for us without taking into consideration the unexpected things along our journey. Many of us find it challenging to adapt to those unforeseen circumstances. I didn't foresee being a teen mom but in actuality it was exactly what I needed to drive me to my purpose-path. My daughter would now become my motivation to succeed, live right, and fight without ceasing.

Although unintended, I was endued with reason. Reason to live, try, and just be. The unexpected is just that, unexpected. Instead of us spending so much time regretting decisions we have made or things we could have done differently...we must learn how to work with where we are and what we have. Trusting and believing that God doesn't make mistakes, even if we do. No matter how traumatic or ugly the situation is, God can turn anything around for his Glory and our success.

My process to discover my purpose was in becoming a mother. I didn't know it right away, but I can tell you that becoming a real life mom is definitely where it started. Purpose was right inside of me and I didn't even know I was pregnant! I always wondered how someone could carry a child for nine months and not notice anything different about themselves. I have two children who are thirteen years apart and, like their personalities, my pregnancies were very dramatic. I couldn't fake them or hide them if I wanted to. I noticed every change in my body. However, that's not everyone's experience. Believe it or not, being oblivious to your own pregnancy is not a myth, it happens more than you may think. Numerous women displayed slight changes like an irregular menstrual cycle that contributed to stress, some gained small amounts of weight but not enough to suggest a baby was on board, and others just felt normal. There are countless testimonies of women going into labor not even realizing they were with-child to begin with.

A lot of why we don't recognize what's going on with our bodies is due to the hustle and bustle of life. It is very easy to become unfocused on our own health and well-being because we are running around taking care of everyone else's needs and wants, rarely taking any time for self-care and self-evaluation. This goes the same for our purpose. We are all walking around pregnant with purpose and promise, not evening recognizing it due to the distractions of our day-to-day survival. Then there are those who may not know they have a well-done bun in the oven because of the information told to them about a misalignment in their reproductive system or that their uterus just isn't strong enough to carry the weight of a child. When these types of adverse statements are spoken over our chances to produce life, it immediately reduces our expectations, brings about discouragement, hopelessness, and resentment. The same type of cause and effect happens with our purpose when people speak death to our dreams instead of life, telling us we aren't smart enough or strong enough.

People have their opinions and point of views, whether professional or nonprofessional, about someone else's ability to dream, aspire, produce, or fulfill their life's purpose. You will hear things like, "Are you sure you heard God tell you that?" "You'll never get the funding for something like that", "Maybe you should try this instead", or "You'll never make enough money to live off of doing that." There are so many more I'm sure you could think of, this is just to name a few. When we take these comments into our ear gates we begin to consciously or subconsciously make it our truth. We hear all these reasons about why we can't do something and we begin to believe other people's opinions over what our heart tells us we can do. Why do we do that to ourselves? I think about how detrimental it is to give another human being that type of power over me, over my thoughts, my drive, and most of all over my will.

Sure, we all like to be encouraged by others and look for advice from those who have been there, done that. However, having the same goal and outcome as someone else doesn't necessarily mean the journey will be the same. We have to walk our own paths and cross our own bridges. Since we are talking about pregnancies in this chapter, let's check out my great grandma's experience. When she had her first baby it was at home with a midwife and no epidural or pain meds. When I had my first baby it was in a fully staffed hospital in a private room and with an epidural. Same results at the end but our deliveries were quite different. I had to come to a place with my purpose-path where I stopped comparing and expecting it to look like someone else's. One of the keys to discovering your purpose is understanding that it is yours! It is for you to manifest it and walk in it, not your friends or your family, but you.

When a woman is introduced to the reality that her desired goal to become a mom is no longer physically possible it's an emotional let down. This is how I felt when I allowed the voices of others to become louder than God's voice, minimizing my potential to be great! I harbored the belief that if I had a purpose it was dead. I killed it with my bad decisions, lack of spiritual progress, and ability to recover in a timely manner. I have always had support and love, so that wasn't my struggle. Self-sabotage was the struggle, emboldening my low self-esteem and need to rebel. I was in my own way of becoming successful. I thought I understood life and knew who I was and where I was going, so instead of waiting on God and listening to wisdom I was trying to do this out of my own intellect. This was a pro and a con for me. The con is I was not always right and because of my bad decision making I delayed my own process. The pro is I developed a drive to succeed. No matter how many people told me I couldn't or even those that said that I could, Mont'ique had to get to the place where she believed there was more for her. As a follower of Christ, I believe what the word of God says about me and His love for me. His promises are YES and AMEN.. I can do all things through Him that strengthens me in spite of what people say and think.

While growing as a mom and caring for my daughter I discovered this selfless human being inside of me. I discovered that I care. I am a person who doesn't just care about being a mom but I care about people. My God given purpose is to serve people, to build them up, and then celebrate their win! I didn't know I was pregnant! Pregnant with purpose! Pregnant with the purpose to selflessly serve!

While serving the needs of my own child something ignited in me to want to help others. I began working in healthcare and my experience obtained from that really exposed the true heart of who I was becoming. I wanted to see others well and healthy. My purpose triggered labor pains when I found myself picking up burdens for other people and utilizing my own resources to help them. I gave away clothes, food, and made monetary donations sometimes out of my capacity. I don't mind getting my hands dirty for others or jumping on a task if I think it is going to help someone else. I genuinely hurt when I see others in some sort of need and I'm not in a position to help them. I was pregnant and I didn't know it!

When I acknowledged this attribute about myself and how it was second nature for me, I discovered my purpose was to selflessly serve and care for others. That was not a learned characteristic; it is just something that was a part of my DNA. At first, I didn't think it was so special. I believed everyone in the world wanted to help in some way but I soon learned about the real world and how selfish people can truly be. Some people serve to gain something in return, others begrudgingly. Sure, we all have the capacity to serve or provide a service, but are we all willing? That's what separates the common server from the one that has a servant's heart.

I always knew I had a purpose just like the little girl I described who played with her dolls and always knew she would be a mom. I just didn't know the how, what, when, and where of my purpose. When the time came to really deliver this hidden ambition inside of me, it caused pain, anxiety, and isolation. It required support and preparation just like a natural delivery would.

The funny thing about what birthing purpose can look like depends on perspective. When a woman is giving birth, from her position, she doesn't see what those on the other side of her bed see unless there is a mirror pointed back at her. She is typically sitting up, looking down, and focusing on the directions of the doctor who is in position to assist. The doctor sees the beauty and all the worst parts of this birthing process but continues to encourage the woman no matter what. Isn't that just like God? Taking in all of our mess and stink while encouraging us to push through, never leaving our side or forsaking our needs. Although we cannot initially see the purpose coming forth from our position, He can see everything at all times from His position. Many of us will get to a place of delivery and want to give up because we are tired. We can't see the crowning of this new life coming forward but it's there and God continues to encourage us to push.

My purpose wasn't discovered in a book or a movie. It was just understanding who I was in Christ and what it meant to be made in His image. I believe that purpose is revealed to us, not taught to us. We are born with it, purpose is in our DNA! Many of us are walking around carrying success and we don't recognize it. Girl, you need to go check with God about what you're carrying! You could be due any day now!

Like many of you, I walked around for way too long with a greater purpose and gift than I ever knew was inside of me until one day I began to experience spiritual labor pains. These are real, I promise you. Spiritual pains hit you naturally in your lower belly and when God is ready to activate you into spiritual motherhood there's nothing you can do about it. No matter your plans, no matter when or how you thought you would be doing it. It's all in God's timing.

In my birthing room is where I discovered why I was created to be in this world. My purpose is to preserve life and save souls. I care about other people outside of myself. I have the heart of a servant. I am Focused & Aligned in All Things God. When I recognized that greater is He that is in me than He that is in the world I became a force to be reckoned with and you can be, too. It shouldn't matter to us where people are in their lives or what their struggles look like, we should be asking God to give us the heart and capacity to reach them, love them, and encourage them to discover their identity and purpose on this Earth.

We also don't have to limit ourselves to one pregnancy. Many of us will go on to birth purpose after purpose, dream after dream, opportunity after opportunity, gift after gift. No matter what you are called to deliver or be a mother to, remember to do it with all your heart and God will provide the increase.

Pain Birthed Purpose

By Engreath Lyna Scharnett

Discovering my Purpose

Of all the places to discover where my life was going, my bed was the place that I would discover my purpose. It happened in October 2019. I was lying in bed talking with my father (God), trying to understand where my life was going and if there was more to my complacent life. At that time, I knew so little about purpose, value, or worth, but I knew that there was more than what was happening at that moment. So, I asked my father what I was supposed to do with all my trauma and pain. What He said jolted me upright!

"Abused, Broken, but Chosen is the name of your nonprofit and you will help hurting women understand that their pain has purpose." That was an AMAZING moment in my life; the discovery that my pain had purpose!

I knew that I needed to understand how to shape the vision for the non-profit that was just given to me, what I did not know was that the purpose birthed in me would need more than just my Father's words. The purpose that was birthed in me would require me to learn how to navigate through the pain, how to lean more into God, what GRACE was, and how to minister forgiveness to me and to others. There was work to do and it would require a mind shift. I was Abused, Broken but I was also Chosen! My life started to make sense, the answers to questions I'd had for years were coming!

I understood that my path was one that I would not have chosen, it was chosen for me. I journeyed in spaces and places that were not very kind, but they were part of my path. The path to becoming the person I was called to be was marked by years of both wisdom and pain. No one else could have walked my path, No one could have journeyed this path with me, it was a solo mission. Since I finally understood my purpose, it was time to do the work! I was able to come to a place, a physical place, that would allow the work to be done so that the healing of others could begin. This journey required so many different tools to do the work. To get the job done God gave me the big guns!

God gave me wisdom. In Proverbs 4v6 (NIV) it says, "Do not forsake wisdom, and she will protect you; love her, and she will watch over you."

He gave me strength. In Philippians 4v13 (KJV) it says, "I can do all things through Christ which strengtheneth me." He also gave me the biggest gun. He taught me the truth of FORGIVENESS! I understood after 4 years of discovering what my purpose was that I needed all those guns to step into the path that was chosen for me. The wisdom would lead me in the right direction to help others continue to heal. This strength would enable me to push through to continue on this path! And, FORGIVENESS is necessary for living, not just existing! Understand that my pain birthed purpose!

In 2015, I arrived in North Carolina, a hot, broken mess. I knew this time would be different because I knew I was going to fight for change. I understood that I wanted something different. I have lived in many states and many more cities and I always ended up back in the place that had broken me, trying to find healing. I did not know that what I was looking for and what I needed would be in a small

Mayberry town. It would be a place of strength, peace, love, and discovery of purpose. I moved several times before moving to North Carolina and there just never seemed to be any peace and then it happened, that shift in the peace, that shift of the mind and that discovery of self-worth and self-value, it was turning, it was shifting and I was about to shift with it!!! I needed to embrace that tool of forgiveness in a way that I never had. I needed to keep leaning and pressing into God. I could look to the hills for that help (Psalm 121). I sat down and wrote 22 letters of forgiveness, it was the hardest thing I had ever done. It was a labored pain that lasted for 2 days!

So, this is where I will help you understand how my pain birthed purpose. The birthing process of my purpose was not like the human birth. The human birth takes approximately 9 months. My birthing purpose was more like an elephant which takes 18 to 23 months. However, my birthing process actually took years and that birth was as painful and as beautiful as the birth of a human being. My pain helped me understand that what has happened to me gives me strength. I help others understand that there is a process for the called of God and God does not equip us to fail. My pain birthed power in my voice and it allowed me to stand on top of all that was on top of me. In writing those 22 letters, it was so freeing. I had broken free through the authentic FORGIVENESS from my heart, I did not want to miss what God had for me, nor do I feel that God would allow me to miss it! Once I got to the last letter, which was to myself, I cried for 2 days. I laid on the couch and I said, "My father, I AM CONTENT!"

I felt that NC was my home and that was 6 years ago. It would take several years for me to unwrap it all and that would come through a support group, some therapy, spiritual counseling and I even took the Freedom class that my church offered. It helped to scrape the rest of the residue of pain after the therapy and support group. I started the path that was chosen for me and I refused to turn around!

PATHWAYS

Pathways chosen-choices not given
Conquering hills and mountain tops of PLEASE, NO, STOP!
Gates of uncertainty followed by fences of fear
Conquering walls and borders of unsure
Roadways of struggles and chaos and tragedy
Passing through the lows of depression valley
Conquering the memories into suppression
These were my pathways they were chosen not given

My Why

I had now shifted my mindset to understand that yes, I suffered horrible life experiences at the hands of others. I had to work through the nightmares. I had to go the distance with counseling and therapy, but that was not the discovery of my purpose, that was the work that needed to be done for myself to get better. Now, after I understood the purpose that was birthed through my rape that happened when I was a 9-year-old child. It took decades to get through that paralyzing pain of rape, the brokenness of trust, and the silence that gripped my tongue to stand on top of all that trauma. My WHY is simple, my WHY is YOU! The hurting you, the powerless you, the you who may be stuck in an emotional place. Your pain makes you feel isolated and alone, it makes you feel unheard and purposeless, as if your voice doesn't matter. You feel as if that darkness is permanent for you. YOU are the reason I do what I do. I was designed by God, chosen by God, and equipped by God to help you understand that you have purpose, you have value, and you matter! My why is to help those who are hurting get through the hurt to the healing! I am now able to understand that in all that I have come through by God's Grace, I was never alone, it only felt that way. God was my help and He was just a prayer away!

I will look to the hills which cometh my help. My help comes from the Lord, which made the heavens and the earth. (Psalm 121v1-2).

Servant Leader

By Shawn Denise Williams Howard

As a servant of the Most High I know I will always win no matter what. However, as a result of a tragedy my life has changed forever. I now live with a health condition: Cardio Myopathy. Beginning in 2014, I was unable to work for six years but during those years God allowed me to spend time with my children. They graduated from High School. My walk with Jesus became stronger. At the same time a close friend of mines had mental health issues so I helped her out. However, she began to attack me. She was threatening to throw my family out of the home we were renting from her. I was terribly shocked because we had been friends for over twelve years, but I didn't know she had been suffering with mental health all of her life. It also taught me to put my trust in God and not men.

I chose to move, but I had no idea where to go. God, who is always there, blessed me with the home that I am currently renting now. I never doubt His love and faithfulness for my family and I. Around that time I had loss my brother from the same heart disease that I am currently been healed from. It was very hurtful and it's still hard to deal with. But will the grace of GOD I am getting through it. My brother will always be my best friend.

How great is our God! After I moved in and got settled (August 2014) I received a text from my friend apologizing for her behavior towards me and my family. I accepted her apology. Sadly, on December 31, 2014, she committed suicide. I was upset by the news of her death but I didn't blame myself; I was always a good friend to her even when she treated me badly. Her death was caused in part by her sickness that obviously caused her great suffering.

Through all of the trials and tribulations, God still gets the glory. I am still here, alive and well. I know that no matter what the task is God will win. I will never give up.

That's when I knew I wanted to serve My father, Jesus, because I always want the best for His people. I always believe His people should have the best in life so I always made myself available to help. It makes me feel good to know I can help. As a child I was pushed to the side by my family, but it didn't change my attitude toward people. I always wondered why I couldn't get the love I gave to people. It really saddens me at times, but with the grace of GOD I still fight to be here on earth. I know I have purpose and it is to help and serve God's people. I don't have suicidal thoughts anymore. With God's strength and love I am getting through it all. I have learned to never put your trust in people, only in GOD always.

ONE TRAGIC NIGHT

July 15, 1991

Life for me was very terrible. At the age of 19, I was brutally mugged by a strange man. It all began in Chicago, Illinois. I had a big dispute with my son's father. I wanted to go home and not be at his parents' house because he was getting high with his brothers. I was really upset with him so I decided to go home. We started fighting so I left. It was midnight on a Friday night. I was so upset with him I wasn't thinking about how late it was or where I was going. I began walking down this dark street. Even though it was only 3 minutes away it seemed like the longest walk ever.

As I proceeded home I became paranoid because it was dark outside and I was walking by myself. What in the world was I thinking? I decided I should turn around. But then again, I was so close to being home that I continued on my 3-minute walk. I walked in front of a motorcycle lounge that was a couple of buildings from where I lived. I started to feel OK but scared at the same time because I knew some of the guys there. My baby's father hung out there and I sold weed to them sometimes. Yes, I was a distributor of weed; that was how I paid the bills in addition to having jobs. I was a telemarketer and he was a hard worker. He could fix anything. I walked home I was approached by one of the men who was a customer of the lounge and he purchased some weed from me. Yes, I actually had some on me because at the time I was fearless of everything and didn't care. I was just that kind of girl.

I continued walking to my apartment and I noticed some strange looking guys I had never seen sitting in the parking lot next to my building. As I made it to my building while searching for my keys I was suddenly grabbed from behind. My heart started racing; I thought my life was over. I tried to scream but it seemed like no words were coming out. I could sense that they were looking for a fight, at least that's what I kept hearing. They were predators. They tried to take my clothes off and then began to beat me in the head. I managed to swing and kick like crazy. I don't know how long that lasted, but I heard a gunshot in the air. Everything went quiet around me. For a few seconds I could hear a man speaking.

"Are you OK? I'm about to call the ambulance," he said. Next thing I knew I was being lifted into the ambulance.

"She's a fighter." Someone said.

"She's lucky," the ambulance guy said.

The next thing I knew, I passed out...I had an encounter with someone standing at the top of the stairs. It was sobering. The voice said, "You're going to be OK."

I also heard my daughter say, "Mom, wake up."

I was awakened by my son's dad asking if I was okay. Next, there were police officers asking me questions; if I remembered my assailants. I couldn't remember anything at all. I was afraid to go outside for weeks which then turned into months, especially because the predators were not caught. That's when I knew I was going to need something to keep me from being paranoid and totally consumed with anxiety. I couldn't sleep or eat some days. I would only go outside in the daytime but I was still fearful. This went on for two years. I already suffered from depression due to losing my daughter's father, Howard Lee Lane, in 1989. His friend shot and killed him. I couldn't go to my mom because she was healing from a nervous breakdown brought on by her divorce. Life was so difficult for me and my family, but I started praying. I didn't know if God would listen to me. I had some bad things happen to me the last three years. Then one day I cried out to God and He heard my cries.

As a child I always knew that I wanted to become a lawyer. However, becoming a mom at 15 presented a lot of challenges that made me feel like I ruined my whole life. I would not listen to my mom but at the same time I was never told about birth control. I felt like it was my parents' fault for not educating me how to protect myself from the unknown. Life happened and I went through a lot of stuff. I found myself in a couple of relationships. It almost killed me being in different relationships with different guys but by the grace of God I am still here. Along the way I ended up pregnant with my second child who has really open my eyes to the fact that I am no longer a teenager. I was a teenage mom with two kids trying to go through my life with them. I knew I loved my kids and would do whatever I could to take care of them and protect them at all cost. I learned a lot and I went through a lot. I was a hustler at all means necessarily too provide I had a weird relationship with my mom but that was something I was so hurt by because I love my mom. She is my forever lady example. My dad was not in the picture because of things that happened between them. My stepfather was wonderful because he helped me with my oldest child but he went away. I still had the thoughts and dreams of becoming a lawyer because I always want God's people to win or fight for their rights. It didn't happen. I ended up with more kids. I thank God for my children; they changed my life. I was able to teach them to dream big, to never give up, and never settle. Most importantly, I taught them to in trust Jesus for everything. I must say I have some amazing kids. I have 16 grandchildren.

Through all my tragedies and sickness, I am still here to talk about it. I even got sick and couldn't work but God still provided. I am 50 years old and I am still standing on God and His promises for my family.

Since 1993 my life has changed. I have been putting God first. I now live in Iowa City, I'm active in a church, and I'm married. God has been healing me from anxiety and depression and I am in business for myself. There are still hard times but they are nothing like what I used to know. I know with His power I can get through them, too.

Amen.

Meet the Authors

Chaundra Nicole Gore. MSL

Chaundra Nicole Gore, MSL is an ordained Minister of the Gospel of Jesus Christ, Affirmed Prophetess, talk show host on the Encouraging Yourself Series LIVE FaceBook/YouTube, Host of Thursday Night at 8 with LensOfFaith LIVE on Facebook/YouTube, servant leadership strategist, destiny catalyst, international speaker, motivational coach/trainer, ghostwriter, #1 Amazon bestselling author, Lens of Faith Speaks, Lens of Faith Speaks Coaching and Consulting, Chancellor of Lens Of Faith Academy of Servant Leadership, CEO of L of F Victorian Militant Prophetic Wear and the Founder and President of Focused and Aligned Women's Business Empowerment Foundation Inc. She is a disabled Army Veteran, as well as a Sexual Assault Victim Advocate, a member of Zeta Phi Beta Sorority Inc, a member Kappa Epsilon Psi Military Sorority Incorporated, a member of the National Society of Success and Leadership, an advocate for Service members as a member of The Association for United States Army, Brand Ambassador for We

Are Women of Substance, Brand Ambassador for Ladies Intentionally Following Through (L.I.F.T), Brand Ambassador for Black Women Handling Business, and Brand Ambassador for Unstoppable Black Women. Outside of all of her professional titles, she is a mother and a survivor of domestic violence and sexual abuse.

Her passion is to help heal people who have suffered abuse, trauma, low self-esteem, doubt, and fear and provide motivation, resources and tools to help them heal and grow.

Chaundra has a Bachelor's of Science in Business Management. A Master's of Science in Leadership. Currently a Doctoral Student at Grand Canyon University pursuing Ed.D (Organizational Leadership). Chaundra is currently a contributing writer in the Aspiring Authors Magazine. Chaundra has been featured in "The Untold Chronicles" Magazine (May 2019 Edition). She has been interviewed on the Dr. Jason Carthen Show, Life Perspectives with Leslie, Dr. Ron Show, Just Daphantly Show, AAALAC Show with Angela Thomas Smith, The Morning Show with Bishop on All Nations Stellar Award-Winning Radio Show, I Am Just Nia Morning Show, Lady Kay Chat Show, Walking In your Purpose with Angela, Triumph Services – Women Transformed, and the Erica Latrice Show. Chaundra authored her first book January 2019 "I Am A Lens Of Faith", after becoming a co-author on her first anthology "We Are Women of Substance". She is also a co-author in "Lift, Launch, Lead", "Unleashing the Roar", co-author in "100 Words of Inspiration", co-author "Queens Supporting Queens" Anthology, "Road to Freedom- Suicide" and the Visionary Author of Focused & Aligned Anthology Part I & II.

Back From Broken Summit - "Be, Know & Do
Black CEO Unstoppable Black Woman Day- The D-Life

The Comeback Champion Summit - Be, Know & Do Leadership Strategy Tips

Success Women's Conference - Illuminating Darkness

I Can See Clearly Summit- Illuminating Darkness

Mental Health Matters Symposium – Illuminating Darkness

Charlene Harrod-Owuamana, AAS. LPN

Charlene Harrod-Owuamana is a Best-selling Author, Professional Speaker and Educator to youth; in Baltimore City. Where she started her business as a "Kid's Coach" for her personal Brand "Nursz's HIVE & CEO/Founder of Owuamana Enterprise, LLC.

She has been in the Healthcare System for over 40+ years. With 20 + years as a Licensed Practical Nurse (LPN); Graduated from Baltimore County Community Colleges (Essex Campus) with an Associate of Science Degree.

She serves on several boards in her city such as: Black Girls Vote (BGV), a Board Member – the Maryland Board of Nursing. Published in several magazines, such as: Entrepreneur 2018 Washington D.C. Edition by Trends and Empowering. Some of her accomplishments includes: Speaking at "Baltimore in Conversation" on Trust VS Mistrust in Healthcare with LGBTQ community; Two-time Speaker at "NursesTakeDC"; Former/Founder of Black Nurses

Rock – Baltimore Maryland Chapter, where she changed lives by educating the communities in which she served. Remaining busy in vulnerable communities doing what God intended her to be nurturing, caring and inspiring Nurse.

I AM A NURSE!!

Melannie F. Hines

Melannie F. Hines is currently a doctoral student at Grand Canyon University studying for her Ed.D in Leadership. She is currently a United States Army Reservist serving her country. Born in Las Vegas, NV and traveled the world ever since. The military has definitely made her a diverse and well-rounded individual. Melannie is a believer of Christ.

Pastor Darlene Hopkins Thorne, MDiv

Darlene Thorne, MDiv, is the CEO of A Heart After the Father, LLC, and serves as your Caregiver's Coach/Mentor. Her mission is to influence change to women ministry leaders teaching them how to practice positive personal self care body, soul and spirit.

As an international speaker Darlene delivers life-impacting messages at conferences and facilitating workshops and symposiums. Featured on television and radio, Darlene focuses on total self care and walking in total freedom and authenticity.

As a published author, Darlene has written several books including participating in two anthologies. Each of her books have been a part of Darlene's journey in leading others to deepen their relationship with God.

She and her husband, Kevin Thorne, serve together as pastors at Renewal Community Church in Clayton, NC. They have two world changer young adults, Kevin, II and Kennedy Elayne. You may contact Darlene Thorne via Instagram.

linktr.ee/Ladydarlene

Author Twanita S. Lassiter, Poet

Twanita Lassiter is a native of Virginia, an U.S. Army veteran, published author, poet and business owner. She is an Amazon Best Selling Author- *Letters to My Husband: Overcoming Adversity through Love, December 2020.* Other publications include *Poetree Growth In Motion, 2015;* and *"A Cup of Coffee,"* a poetry piece published in *"The Colors of Life"* book by the International Library of Poetry.

In 2017, Twanita created Poetree Growth In Motion, LLC (P.G.I.M.). She specializes in creative and therapeutic writing and vision board workshops. The purpose behind P.G.I.M. is to connect with individuals on a personal level while acknowledging that each of us experience similar situations, exert different responses, and yield different outcomes. Twanita creates intimate settings for both workshops allowing individuals to become vulnerable in a safe environment expressing strengths, weaknesses, and fears. She annually hosts youth conferences to equip youth with tools to combat adversity (personal, environmental, relationship).

Author Mia Monique

AUTHOR
ADVOCATE
LIFECOACH

Author Mia Monique is a Bestselling Author, life Coach, Domestic Violence advocate, Motivational Speaker, and life strategist. Mia began her career in 2011 as a Domestic violence advocate. Mia a former victim of Domestic violence and Emotional abuse, decided to use her voice and story for her community and Works with Women, Men and Children who face the same perils she did as a child and into her adult years.

Mia was the Keynote Speaker in Johnstown PA at an annual Walking in Her Shoes event (2011) standing up against violence against women. She then founded her own Organization Unbreakable LLC which helps victims of abuse.

In 2016 Mia signed a publishing deal with Mystery Eyes Publications Releasing her first book Conflicted: Recognizing Generational Curses And breaking free and went on to publish Devil in the Mirror: Escaping the narcissistic relationship 101. Her latest Focused and Aligned an Anthology Mia discussed how she became Focused and Aligned sharing again her passion to use her voice to uplift and motivate people to live their lives in their purpose and push beyond their pain.

Mia is also Founder of Meaningful Impact Association M.I.A with Meaningful Impact Association she is gaining unparalleled experience in the healing of victims of childhood trauma, and abuse while also establishing herself as a respected and trusted leader in her community. Mia is Currently working on her very own Magazine Publication Titled Meaningful Impact Magazine where she showcases various pillars, entrepreneurs, philanthropist, and activist in her community and across the world.

Mia is setting a new standard for how healing from childhood trauma and abuse can be changed and addressed in our communities and society. Her commitment and dedication is changing lives daily. She uses her platform to educate and enlighten listeners on her Podcast Conversation and Clarity with Mia Monique.

Prophetess Montique "Honeybee" Moore

Fire Lieutenant, Founder of All Things God Inc., Public Speaker, Entrepreneur, Philanthropist and Professional Certified Leader.

As a Professional Certified Leader Montique has gone from following the leader to leading the room. Montique is passionate about teaching others to overcome their fears and manifest the purpose they have within. As a 15 year veteran Fire Lieutenant, Montique has been faced with a variety of challenges regarding race, gender equality, and ability to lead in a male dominated field. In the face of what should have made her quit and give up she prevailed and elevated into her purpose.

Montique believes that her time as a Firefighter is part of her purpose-path. It is those experiences that helped shape her and propel her into her purpose of being a servant leader. Outside of serving in her community as a Firefighter/EMT she also volunteered as a Connecticut Ambassador for Black Girls Run encouraging and challenging women to establish fitness goals and stay committed to them. Montique served as a dance team coach where she not only taught dance but mentored youth by teaching life skills and establishing education goals.

Montique has been awarded the 100 Women of Color award along with citations from the State of Connecticut for her great community work as well as her ability to minister and lead women throughout the Globe in her workshops, women conferences, live social media "Bible Talks" and her All Things God Podcast " It's More Than a Podcast" across the Globe. Montique is not just   another voice wanting to be heard but a transcending instrument for those who whisper, those who have been muzzled and those who desire to be heard.

In all her many awards, recognitions and citations the one she holds close to her heart is the

City of Bridgeport Recognition for her life-saving efforts that saved a 10 month old child's life.

Outside of her public service career, Montique is the CEO/Founder of All Things God Inc. which is a charitable organization focused on social-being and philanthropy.

While juggling it all Montique is a dedicated wife to her husband of ten years and mother of two God sent daughters. She has been chosen by God to save lives in the natural and in the spirit.

Engreath Lyna Scharnett

I am Queen Engreath Lyna Scharnett, I took my 1st God-given breath on March 27, 1964 to an awesome Woman of God, Juanita Myles-Scharnett. I experienced my first heartbreak, before I took my first step, from my father; who disappeared shortly after my birth. As life would have it, that would be the first of many heartbreaks and those heartbreaks and valley experience would become stepping stones to lessons in life, for me. Having lived most of my life in Baton Rouge, LA. as it turned out, would be the same place where most of my valley experiences would take place. I attended Grambling State University majoring in Psychology, where devastation would be the hiccup to obtaining my degree. I would move past and survive those devastating experiences and raise 2 amazing sons, gain 1 beautiful daughter-in-law, who would bless me with 5 very beautiful grandchildren. And, now after years of being broken and angry I am now living and thriving in North Carolina, building my God-given non-profit Abused Broken but Chosen. I am walking the path that was paved for me by GOD, by the battles I have won and the wars I have overcome.

I AM...QUEEN ENGREATH LYNA SCHARNETT

Shawn Denise Williams Howard

Re'zilyant is my Name
Shawn Williams Howard

Birthday: May 24, 1971
Born: Chicago, Illinois
Siblings: 7 siblings, 3 sisters and 4 brothers
Parent: Betty Williams, Plato Townsend

Interesting facts: I love Jesus. Her spiritual gifts are evangelism, servant heart, mercy. Mother of 6 boys and 2 girls in addition to 16 grandchildren. Married to Melvin A Howard for nearly six years. Entrepreneur, Director in Sales, Total Life Charger

Minister Keywana Wright-Jones

Minister Keywana Wright-Jones is a devoted wife and mother.

She is a native of Flint, Michigan. She is an Amazon Best Selling Author, Radio and Podcast host,

Life coach, and Prayer warrior.

She self-published her first book, "Walking in God Destiny". She served as the prayer intercessor for the Focused & Aligned the birthing room book project.